How Should *I Live* in This World?

The Crucial Questions Series By R.C. Sproul

Who *Is* Jesus?

Can I Trust *the* Bible?

Does *Prayer* Change Things?

Can I *Know* God's Will?

How Should I *Live* in This World?

What Does It Mean *to Be* Born Again?

Can I Be Sure *I'm* Saved?

What *Is* Faith?

What Can I *Do with* My Guilt?

What *Is the* Trinity?

What *Is* Baptism?

Can I Have *Joy in* My Life?

Who Is *the* Holy Spirit?

Does God *Control* Everything?

How Can I Develop a Christian Conscience?

What *Is the* Lord's Supper?

What Is *the* Church?

What *Is* Repentance?

What Is *the Relationship between* Church *and* State?

Are These *the* Last Days?

What *Is the* Great Commission?

Can I *Lose My* Salvation?

Free digital editions available at ReformationTrust.com/FreeCQ

CRUCIAL
QUESTIONS
No. | 5

How Should *I Live*
in This World?

R.C. Sproul

R *Reformation Trust*   A DIVISION OF LIGONIER MINISTRIES, ORLANDO, FL

How Should I Live in This World?

© 1983, 1999, 2009, 2010 by R. C. Sproul

Previously published as *Ethics and the Christian* (1983) and as part of *Following Christ* (1991) by Tyndale House Publishers, and as *How Should I Live in This World?* by Ligonier Ministries (1999).

Published by Reformation Trust Publishing
a division of Ligonier Ministries
421 Ligonier Court, Sanford, FL 32771
Ligonier.org   ReformationTrust.com

Printed in North Mankato, MN
Corporate Graphics
August 2015
First edition, sixth printing

Cover design: Gearbox Studios
Interior design and typeset: Katherine Lloyd, The DESK

Library of Congress Cataloging-in-Publication Data
Sproul, R. C. (Robert Charles), 1939-
[Ethics and the Christian]
How should I live in this world? / R. C. Sproul.
p. cm. -- (The crucial questions series)

First published as: Ethics and the Christian, 1983. Following Christ. Wheaton, Ill. : Tyndale House Publishers, 1991. How should I live in this world? Ligonier Ministries, 1999.
ISBN 978-1-56769-180-1
1. Christian ethics. I. Sproul, R. C. (Robert Charles), 1939- Following Christ. II. Title.
BJ1251.S67 2009
241--dc22

2009018824

Contents

Preface

Almost every major discussion of ethics these days begins with an analysis of the chaotic situation of modern culture. Even secular writers and thinkers are calling for some sort of basic agreement on ethical behavior. Humanity's "margin of error," they say, is shrinking with each new day. Our survival is at stake.

These "prophets of doom" point out that man's destructive capability increased from 1945 to 1960 by the same ratio as it did from the primitive weapons of the Stone Age to the dropping of the atomic bomb on Hiroshima. The thawing of the Cold War provided little comfort. Numerous nations have nuclear arms now or are close to having them. What, besides ethics, will keep them from using these weapons?

This stark reality is compounded by the profusion of social injustice in many areas, the rise of international terrorism, and the general decline of personal and social values.

Who is to say what's right and wrong? One technical volume, Thomas E. Hill's *Contemporary Ethical Theories*, lists more than eighty theories of ethics competing for acceptance in our modern world. It is not just a matter of "doing the right thing" but of figuring out what the right thing is. This proliferation of options generates confusion in our world and, for many, a sense of despair. Will we ever reach a cultural consensus that will stabilize the shifting sands of pluralism?

All this talk of "theories of ethics" may leave you cold. However, ethical decisions enter into every aspect of our lives. No field or career is immune from ethical judgments. In politics, in psychology, and in medicine, ethical decisions are made regularly. Legislative action, economic policy, academic curricula, psychiatric advice—all involve ethical considerations. Every vote cast in the ballot box marks an ethical decision.

On what basis should we make these decisions? That's where the "ethical theories" come in. The Christian may say, "I simply obey God's Word." However, what about those issues where the Bible has no specific "thou shalt"? Can we find ethical principles in Scripture, and in the very nature of God, that will guide us through this difficult terrain? How can we communicate these principles to others?

How does God's Word stand up against the eighty-some other standards?

Let us start by looking deeper into the field of ethics to consider how society deals with such questions. Then we will see how God's Word fits in, and we will seek to apply biblical teaching to several modern dilemmas.

Chapter One

ETHICS
AND MORALS

In present word usage, the term *ethics* is often used interchangeably with the word *morality*. That the two have become virtual synonyms is a sign of the confusion that permeates the modern ethical scene. Historically, the two words had quite distinctive meanings. *Ethics* comes from the Greek *ethos*, which is derived from a root word meaning "stall," a place for horses. It conveyed the sense of a dwelling place, a place of stability and permanence. On the other hand, *morality* comes from the word *mores*, which describes the behavioral patterns of a given society.

Ethics is a normative science, searching for the principal foundations that prescribe obligations or "oughtness." It is concerned primarily with the imperative and with the philosophical premises on which imperatives are based. *Morality* is a descriptive science, concerned with "isness" and the indicative. Ethics define what people ought to do; morals describe what people actually do. The difference between them is between the normal and the descriptive.

ETHICS	MORALS
1. normative	1. descriptive
2. imperative	2. indicative
3. oughtness	3. isness
4. absolute	4. relative

When morality is identified with ethics, the descriptive becomes the normative and the imperative is swallowed by the status quo. This creates a kind of "statistical morality." In this schema, the good is determined by the normal and the normal is determined by the statistical average. The "norm" is discovered by an analysis of the normal, or by counting noses. Conformity to that norm then becomes the ethical obligation. It works like this:

Step 1. We compile an analysis of statistical behavior patterns, such as those integral to the groundbreaking Kinsey Reports in the twentieth century. If we discover that most people are participating in premarital sexual intercourse, then we declare such activity "normal."

Step 2. We move quickly from the normal to a description of what is authentically "human." Humanness is defined by what human beings do. Hence, if the normal human being engages in pre-marital sexual intercourse, we conclude that such activity is normal and therefore "good."

Step 3. The third step is to declare patterns that deviate from the normal to be abnormal, inhuman, and inauthentic. In this schema, chastity becomes a form of deviant sexual behavior and the stigma is placed on the virgin rather than the nonvirgin.

Statistical morality operates according to the following syllogism:

Premise A—the normal is determined by statistics;
Premise B—the normal is human and good;
Conclusion—the abnormal is inhuman and bad.

In this humanistic approach to ethics, the highest good is defined as that activity that is most authentically human. This method achieves great popularity when applied to some issues but breaks down when applied to others. For instance, if we do a statistical analysis of the experience of cheating among students or lying among the general public, we discover that a majority of students have at some time cheated and that everyone has at some time lied. If the canons of statistical morality apply, the only verdict we can render is that cheating is an authentically human good and that lying is a bona fide virtue.

Obviously there must be a relationship between our ethical theories and our moral behavior. In a real sense, our beliefs dictate our behavior. A theory underlies our every moral action. We may not be able to articulate that theory or even be immediately conscious of it, but nothing manifests our value systems more sharply than our actions.

The Christian ethic is based on an antithesis between what is and what ought to be. We view the world as fallen; an analysis of fallen human behavior describes what is normal to the abnormal situation of human corruption. God calls us out of the indicative by His imperative. Ours is a call to nonconformity—to a transforming ethic that shatters the status quo.

A Serious Inconsistency

Even within relativistic claims, a serious inconsistency emerges. The 1960s brought a moral revolution to our culture, spearheaded by the protests of the youth. Two slogans were repeated, broadcast side by side during this movement. The tension was captured by these twin slogans: "Tell it like it is" and "Do your own thing."

The cry for personal freedom was encapsulated in the "inalienable right" to do one's own thing. This was a demand for subjective freedom of self-expression. When the guns were turned on the older generation, however, a curious and glaring inconsistency was heard: "Tell it like it is." This slogan implies an objective basis for truth and virtue. The adult generation was not "allowed" to do their own thing if doing their own thing deviated from objective norms of truth. The flower children demanded the right to have their ethical cake and eat it too.

I was once maneuvered into an unenviable counseling

situation by a distraught Christian mother, a modern-day Monica (mother of Augustine) anguishing over the wayward behavior of her nonbelieving and rebellious son. The lad had retreated from his mother's constant religious and moral directives by moving out of the family home and into his own apartment. He promptly decorated his apartment with black walls and strobe lights, then adorned the room with accoutrements designed for the liberal indulgence of hashish and other exotic drugs. His was a bacchanalian "pad" into which he promptly invited a willing coed to join him in luxurious cohabitation. All of this was to his mother's unmitigated horror. I agreed to talk with the young man only after explaining to the mother that such an encounter would probably engender further hostility. I would be viewed as the mother's "hired gun." The youth also agreed to the meeting, obviously only to escape further verbal harassment from his mother.

When the young man appeared at my office, he was overtly hostile and obviously wanted to get the meeting over with as quickly as possible. I began the interview bluntly by asking directly, "Who are you mad at?"

Without hesitation he growled, "My mother."

"Why?" I inquired.

"Because all she does is hassle me. She keeps trying to shove religion down my throat."

I went on to inquire what alternative value system he had embraced in place of his mother's ethical system. He replied, "I believe everyone ought to be free to do his own thing."

I then asked, "Does that include your mother?" He was startled by the question and not immediately aware of what I was driving at. I explained to him that if he embraced a Christian ethic, he could readily enlist me as an ally in his cause. His mother had been harsh, provoking her son to wrath and being insensitive to questions and feelings, issues that are indeed circumscribed by the biblical ethic. I explained that at several crucial points his mother had violated Christian ethics. However, I pointed out that on the boy's ethical terms he had no legitimate gripe. "Maybe your mother's 'thing' is to harass children by shoving religion down their throats," I said. "How can you possibly object to that?" It became clear that the boy wanted everybody (especially himself) to have the right to do his or her "own thing" except when the other person's "thing" impinged on *his* "thing."

It is commonplace to hear the lament that some Christians, notably conservatives, are so rigidly bound by moralistic guidelines that everything becomes for them a matter of "black and white" with no room for "gray" areas.

Those who persist in fleeing from the gray, seeking refuge in the sharply defined areas of white and black, suffer from the epithets "brittle" or "dogmatic." However, the Christian must seek for righteousness and never be satisfied with living in the smog of perpetual grayness. He wants to know where the right way is located, where the path of righteousness lies.

There is a right and there is a wrong. The difference between them is the concern of ethics. We seek a way to find the *right*, which is neither subjective nor arbitrary. We seek norms and principles that transcend prejudice or mere societal conventions. We seek an objective basis for our ethical standards. Ultimately we seek a knowledge of the character of God, whose holiness is to be reflected in our patterns of behavior. With God there is a definite and absolute black and white. The problem for us is to discover which things belong where. The following chart depicts our dilemma:

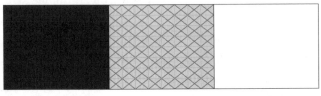

SIN   VIRTUE

The black section represents sin or unrighteousness. The white section represents virtue or righteousness. What does the gray represent? The gray area may call attention to two different problems of Christian ethics. First, it may be used to refer to those activities the Bible describes as *adiaphorous*. Adiaphorous matters are those things that, in themselves, are ethically neutral. Such matters as eating food offered to idols are placed in this category. Adiaphorous matters are not sinful, but there are occasions when they might become sinful. Ping-Pong playing, for example, is not sinful. However, if a person becomes obsessed with Ping-Pong to the extent that it dominates his life, it becomes a sinful thing for that person.

The second problem represented by the gray area is more important for us to grasp. Here, the gray area represents *confusion*: it encompasses those matters where we are uncertain about what is right and wrong. The presence of gray calls attention to the fact that ethics is not a simple science but a complex one. Finding the black and the white areas is a noble concern. Jumping to them simplistically, however, is devastating to the Christian life. When we react to black/white approaches to ethics, we may be accurately assessing an annoying human tendency toward simplistic thinking. But we must guard against leaping to the conclusion that there are no areas where black/white thinking is valid. Only within the context of atheism can we speak of there being no black and white. We desire competent and consistent theism, which demands a rigorous scrutiny of ethical principles in order to find our way out of the confusion of the gray.

The Ethical Continuum

Our graph also may be used to illustrate the ethical continuum. In classical terms, sin is described as righteousness run amok. Evil is seen as the negation, privation, or distortion of the good. Man was created to labor in a garden. In modern jargon, the workplace is described as a jungle. What is the difference between a garden and a jungle? A jungle is merely a chaotic garden, a garden run wild.

Man was created with an aspiration for significance, which is a virtue. Man can pervert that drive into a lust for power, which is a vice. These represent the two poles on the continuum. At some point, we cross a line between virtue and vice. The closer we come to that line, the more difficult it is for us to perceive it clearly and the more our minds encounter the foggy gray area.

While teaching a course on ethics to clergymen working

on doctor of ministry degrees, I posed the following ethical dilemma: A husband and wife are interned in a concentration camp. They are housed in separate quarters with no communication between them. A guard approaches the wife and demands that she have sexual intercourse with him. The wife refuses. The guard then declares that unless the woman submits to his overtures, he will have her husband shot. The woman submits. When the camp is liberated and the husband learns of his wife's behavior, he sues her for divorce on the grounds of adultery.

I then posed this question to twenty conservative clergymen: "Would you grant the man a divorce on the grounds of adultery?" All twenty answered yes, pointing to the obvious fact that the wife did have sexual relations with the guard. They saw extenuating circumstances in the situation, but the situation did not change the fact of the wife's immoral behavior.

I then asked, "If a woman is forcibly raped, may the husband sue for divorce on the grounds of adultery?" All twenty responded no. The clergymen all recognized a clear distinction between adultery and rape. The difference is found at the point of coercion versus voluntary participation. I pointed out that the prison guard used coercion (forcing the wife's compliance lest the husband be killed) and asked whether the woman's "adultery" was not actually rape.

By my mere raising of the question, half of the clergymen changed their verdict. After prolonged discussion, almost all of them did. The presence of the element of coercion threw the adultery issue into the gray area of confusion. Even those who did not completely change their minds strongly modified their decisions to account for the extenuating circumstances, which moved the woman's "crime" from the clear area of sin into the gray area of complexity. They all agreed that if it was sin, it was a lesser sin than adultery committed with "malice aforethought."

That a continuum exists between virtue and vice was the main thrust of Jesus' teaching in the Sermon on the Mount. He was teaching the principle of the complex of righteousness and the complex of sin. The Pharisees had embraced a simplistic understanding of the Ten Commandments. Their ethical judgments were superficial and therefore distorted. They failed to grasp the continuum motif.

I once read an article by a prominent psychiatrist who was critical of Jesus' ethical teaching. He expressed astonishment that the Western world had been so laudatory about Jesus as a "great teacher." He pointed to the Sermon on the Mount (Matt. 5–7) as exhibit A for the foolishness of Jesus' ethical teaching. He asked why we extol the wisdom of a teacher who held that it is just as bad for a man to lust after a woman as it is to commit adultery with her. He questioned how a teacher could argue that it is just as bad to be angry at a man or to call him a fool as it is to murder him. He then belabored the difference between the destruction caused by lust as opposed to adultery and that caused by slander as opposed to murder.

The answer to the psychiatrist should be clear. Jesus did not teach that lust was as bad as adultery or that anger was as bad as murder. (Unfortunately, many Christians have jumped to the same erroneous conclusion as the psychiatrist, obscuring the point of Jesus' ethical teaching.)

Jesus was correcting the simplistic view of the law held by the Pharisees. They had embraced an "everything but" philosophy of technical morality, assuming that if they avoided the most obvious dimension of the commandments, they fulfilled the law. Like the rich young ruler, they had a simplistic and external understanding of the Decalogue. Because they had never actually murdered anyone, they thought they had kept the law perfectly. Jesus spelled out the wider implications or the complex of the law. "You shall not kill" means more than refraining from homicide. It prohibits the entire complex that goes into murder. It also implies its opposite virtue: "You shall promote life." In our continuum, we see the following range:

```
VICE --------------------------------- VIRTUE

Murder-Hatred-Slander --------------- Saving Life
Destroying Life --------------------- Promoting Life
```

A similar continuum moves from the vice of adultery to the virtue of chastity. In between are lesser virtues and lesser sins, but virtues and sins nonetheless.

Jesus' teaching revealed both the spirit and the letter of the law. For instance, slander doesn't kill the body or leave the wife a widow and the children orphans. It does destroy a man's good name, which robs him of a quality aspect of life. Slander murders the man "in spirit." The Pharisees had become crass literalists, ignoring the spirit of the law and missing the wider concerns of the complex of the sin of murder.

Degrees of Sin?

To speak of an ethical continuum or a complex of righteousness and evil is to plunge us into the debate over degrees of sin and righteousness. The Bible teaches that if we sin against one point of the law, we sin against the whole law. Does this not imply that sin is sin and that ultimately there are no degrees? Has not Protestantism repudiated the Roman Catholic distinction between mortal and venial sins? These are the issues that come to the surface as soon as we begin to speak of degrees of sin.

Certainly the Bible teaches that if we sin against one point of the law we sin against the whole law (James 2:10), but we must not infer from this that there are no degrees of sin. Sinning against the law is sinning against the God of the law. When I violate one point of God's law, I bring myself into opposition to God Himself. This is not to say that sinning against one point of the law is the equivalent of sinning against five points of the law. In both cases, I violate the law and do violence to God, but the frequency of my violence is five times as great in the latter as in the former.

It is true that God commands perfect obedience to the whole law, so that by a single transgression I stand exposed to His judgment. The lightest sin exposes me to the wrath of God, for in the smallest peccadillo I am guilty of cosmic treason. In the least transgression, I set myself above the authority of God, doing insult to His majesty, His holiness, and His sovereign right to govern me. Sin is a revolutionary act in which the sinner seeks to depose God from His throne. Sin is a presumption of supreme arrogance in that the creature vaunts his own wisdom above that of the Creator, challenges divine omnipotence with human impotence, and seeks to usurp the rightful authority of the cosmic Lord.

It is true that historical Protestantism has rejected the Roman Catholic schema of mortal and venial sins. The rejection, however, is not based on a rejection of degrees of sin. John Calvin, for example, argued that all sin is mortal in the sense that it rightly deserves death, but that no sin is mortal in the sense that it destroys justifying grace. Considerations other than the degrees of sin were in view in the Protestant rejection of the mortal and venial sin distinction. Historical Protestantism retained the distinction between ordinary sins and sins that are deemed gross and heinous.

The most obvious reason for the Protestant retention of degrees of sin is that the Bible abounds with such gradations. The Old Testament law had clear distinctions and penalties for different criminal acts. Some sins were punishable by death, others by corporal penalties, and still others by the levying of fines. In the Jewish criminal justice system, distinctions were made between types of murder that would correspond to modern-day distinctions such as first- and second-degree murder, and voluntary and involuntary manslaughter.

The New Testament lists certain sins that, if continued in impenitence, demand the forfeiture of Christian fellowship (1 Cor. 5). At the same time, the New Testament advocates a kind of love that covers a multitude of sins (1 Peter 4:8). Warnings abound concerning a future judgment that will take into account both the number (quantity) and the severity (quality) of our sins. Jesus speaks of those who will receive many stripes and those who will receive few (Luke 12:44–48, KJV); of the comparatively greater judgment that will befall Chorazin and Bethsaida as opposed to Sodom (Matt. 11:20–24); and the greater and lesser degree of rewards that will be distributed to the saints. The apostle Paul warns the Romans against heaping up wrath against the day of God's wrath (Rom. 2:5). These and a host of other passages indicate that God's judgment will be perfectly just, measuring the number, the severity, and the extenuating circumstances that attend all of our sins.

Chapter Two

REVEALED
ETHICS

At the heart of Christian ethics is the conviction that our firm basis for knowing the true, the good, and the right is divine revelation. Christianity is not a life system that operates on the basis of speculative reason or pragmatic expediency. We assert boldly that God has revealed to us who He is, who we are, and how we are expected to relate to Him. He has revealed for us that which is pleasing to Him and commanded by Him. Revelation provides a supernatural aid in understanding the good. This point is so basic and so obvious that it has often been overlooked and obscured as we search for answers to particular questions.

The departure from divine revelation has brought our culture to chaos in the area of ethics. We have lost our basis of knowledge, our epistemological foundation, for discovering the good. This is not to suggest that God has given us a codebook that is so detailed in its precepts that all ethical decisions are easy. That would be a vast oversimplification of the truth. God has not given us specific instructions for each and every possible ethical issue we face, but neither are we left to grope in the dark and to make our decisions on the basis of mere opinion. This is an important comfort to the Christian because it assures us that in dealing with ethical questions, we are never working in a vacuum. The ethical decisions that we make touch the lives of people, and mold and shape human personality and character. It is precisely at this point that we need the assistance of God's superior wisdom.

To be guided by God's revelation is both comforting and risky. It is comforting because we can rest in the assurance that our ethical decisions proceed from the mind of One whose wisdom is transcendent. God's law not only reflects His righteous character but manifests His infinite wisdom. His knowledge of our humanity and His grasp of our needs for fullness of growth and development far exceed the collective wisdom of all of the world's greatest thinkers. Psychiatrists will never understand the human psyche to the degree the Creator understands that which He made. God knows our frames; it is He who has made us so fearfully and wonderfully. All of the nuances and complexities that bombard our senses and coalesce to produce a human personality are known in their intimate details by the divine mind.

Taking comfort in divine revelation is risky business. It is risky precisely because the presence of hostility in the human heart to the rule of God makes for conflict between divine precepts and human desires. To take an ethical stand on the foundation of divine revelation is to bring oneself into serious and at times radical conflict with the opinions of men. Every day, clergymen around the world give counsel and advice that run contrary to the clear mandates of God. How can we explain such a separation between God's Word and ministerial counsel?

One critical factor in this dilemma is the fact that ministers are profoundly pressed to conform to acceptable contemporary standards. The person who comes to the minister for counsel is not always looking for guidance from a transcendent God, but rather for permission to do what he or she wants—a license to sin. The Christian counselor is vulnerable to sophisticated forms of manipulation coming from the very people who seek his advice. The minister is placed in that difficult pressure point of acquiescing to the desires of the people or being considered unloving and fun-squelching. Add to this the cultural emphasis that there is something dehumanizing in the discipline and moral restraints God imposes on us. Thus, to stand with God is often to stand against men and to face the fiery trials that go with Christian convictions.

Ethics involves the question of authority. The Christian lives under the sovereignty of God, who alone may claim lordship over us. Christian ethics is theocentric as opposed to secular or philosophical ethics, which tend to be anthropocentric. For the humanist, man is the norm, the ultimate standard of behavior. Christians, however, assert that God is the center of all things and that His character is the absolute standard by which questions of right and wrong are determined.

Theonomy, Autonomy, Heteronomy

The sovereignty of God deals not only with abstract principles but with real lines of authority. God has the right to issue commands, to impose obligations, and to bind the consciences of men. Christians live in the context of theonomy. Debates about law and ethics tend to focus on two basic options—autonomy and heteronomy. Autonomy declares that man is a law unto himself. The autonomous man creates his own value system and establishes his own norms, and is answerable and accountable to man and to man alone. Heteronomy means "ruled by another." In any system of heteronomy, the individual is considered to be morally responsible to obey limits and proscriptions imposed on him by someone else. This someone else might be another individual, a group such as the state, or even a transcendent God. When we speak of theonomy, or the rule of God, we are speaking of a specific kind of heteronomy. Theonomy is rule by another who is identified as God. This distinction between autonomy and theonomy is the most fundamental conflict of mankind. When theonomy is abandoned for autonomy, the biblical description of that action is sin. It is the creature's declaration of independence from his Creator.

There is an important difference between freedom and autonomy. Though autonomy is a kind of freedom, it carries the dimensions of freedom to the level of the absolute. Christianity asserts that God gives man freedom, but that freedom has limits. Our freedom never moves us to the point of autonomy. Some have viewed the fall of man in Eden as a result of man's primordial grasp for autonomy—man's basal sin, the attempt to usurp the authority that belongs to God.

Friedrich Nietzsche, in trying to locate the most basic of human characteristics, located it in what he called man's lust or will to power. For Nietzsche, the authentic man was the one who refused to submit to the herd morality of the masses—an existential hero who had the courage to create his own values. For man to create his own values absolutely, the first thing he must do is to declare the death of God. As long as God exists, He represents the ultimate threat to man's pretended autonomy. Jean-Paul Sartre also addressed this theme when he declared that unless freedom reaches the full measure of autonomy, it is not true freedom. Thus, Sartre stands with those who would dismiss God from the ethical arena.

In the United States, our concept of liberty has changed drastically from the eighteenth century to the twenty-first century. The change has much to do with our understanding of autonomy. Modern man considers the quest for autonomy to be a noble and virtuous declaration of human creativity. From the Christian vantage point, however, the quest for autonomy represents the essence of evil, as it contains within its agenda the assassination of God.

The contemporary existentialist cries that "cowering in the shadow of the Almighty" is the worst thing man can do. Such human dependency on divine assistance, he says, encourages weakness and inevitable decadence. To be sure, many people flee to Christianity because of moral weakness, but the fundamental issue is not what we regard to be preferable states of mind or psychological attitudes. The ultimate issue centers on the existence of God. It matters not whether I enjoy submitting to God. What matters first is the question, "Is there a God?" Without God, the only possible end of ethical reflection is chaos. Fyodor Dostoevsky captured this idea in *The Brothers Karamazov*, where one of his characters says, "If there is no God, all things are permissible."

The God of Christianity is sovereign, wise, righteous, and ultimately concerned with justice. Not only is God concerned with justice, He assumes the role of Judge over us. It is axiomatic to Christianity that our actions will be judged. This theme is conspicuously absent in much Christian teaching today, yet it fills the New Testament and touches virtually every sermon of Jesus of Nazareth. We will be called into account for every idle word we speak. On the final day, it will not be our consciences that will accuse or excuse us, but God Himself.

Christian ethics cannot be established in a vacuum. The Christian is not concerned with ethics for ethics' sake. We understand that rules for conduct are established in the context of God's will for human redemption. There is a real sense in which grace precedes law. The very giving of commandments by the Creator is in the context of a covenant that God makes on the basis of grace. The purpose of divine commandments is redemption. The law of the Old Testament and of the New Testament is fundamentally person-oriented. To isolate this law from its basic concern for people is to fall into the abyss of legalism. Christian ethics is built on the obedience of people to a personal God. When God first gave the law, He did so by means of a personal introduction: "*I am* the LORD *your* God, who brought *you* out of the land of Egypt, out of the house of slavery. *You* shall have no other gods before *me*. *You* shall not . . ." (Ex. 20:2–4a, emphasis added). We see that this is not law for law's sake, but for people's sake.

Chapter Three

LEGALISM AND
ANTINOMIANISM

The continuum of ethics is divided sharply by a fine line, the razor's edge. This fine line of demarcation is similar to what Jesus described as the "narrow way." The New Testament makes frequent reference to Christians living according to "the way." Christians in the first century were called "people of the way." Jesus called His disciples to walk by the narrow way and enter by the straight gate that leads to life, while warning against the broad way that leads to destruction (Matt. 7:13–14). However, there is a difference between a narrow way and narrow-mindedness. Narrow-mindedness reveals a judgmental attitude, a critical mindset, which is far from the biblical ideal of charity. Walking the narrow way involves not a distorted mental attitude but a clear understanding of what righteousness demands.

One can deviate from the path of righteousness by moving too far to the left or to the right. One can stumble from the narrow way by falling off the road in either direction. If we consider ethics again in terms of the model of the continuum, we know that the opposite poles, which represent distortions of authentic righteousness, may be labeled legalism and antinomianism. These twin distortions have plagued the church as long as it has been in existence. The New Testament documents reveal that struggles with both legalism and antinomianism were common in the New Testament church.

Legalism Found in Many Forms

Legalism is a distortion that takes many forms. The first form of legalism involves the abstracting of the law of God from its original context. This variety of legalism reduces Christianity to a list of do's and don'ts, a codified system of rigid moralism that is divorced from the covenant context of love. To be sure, God gives rules. He pronounces do's and don'ts, but the purpose of these rules is to describe for us what is pleasing and displeasing to God. God is concerned with the heart attitude that one brings with him to the application of the rules. When the rules are kept for their own sake, obedience is given to a cold abstraction known as the law rather than to a personal God who reveals the law.

A second dimension of legalism, closely related to the first, involves the divorce of the letter of the law from the spirit of the law. This is the distortion Jesus constantly dealt with when confronting the Pharisees, and He rebuked them for it in the Sermon on the Mount. As we have indicated with respect to Jesus' expansion of the full import of the law in the Sermon on the Mount, it is not enough for the godly person to obey the mere externals of the law while ignoring the deeper implications of the spirit behind the law. The Pharisees became masters of external obedience coupled with internal disobedience.

The distinction between spirit and letter touches the question of motive. When the Bible describes goodness, it does so in a complex way. Some are offended by the universal indictment brought against fallen mankind, which Paul articulates in his epistle to the Romans. The apostle declares that "none is righteous, no, not one; . . . no one does good, not even one"

(Rom. 3:10, 12). Here the apostle echoes the radical statement with which Jesus replied to the question of the rich young ruler: "Why do you call me good? No one is good except God alone" (Mark 10:18). At face value, the Bible seems to teach that no one ever does a good thing in this world. This is a grim evaluation of the conduct of fallen human beings.

How are we to understand this radical judgment of human ethical conduct? The key is to be found in an analysis of the biblical definition of the good. For an action to be judged good by God, it must fulfill two primary requirements. The first is that the action must correspond outwardly to the demands of the law. Second, the inward motivation for the act must proceed from a heart that is altogether disposed toward the glory of God. It is the second dimension, the spiritual dimension of motive, that prevents so many of our deeds from being evaluated as good. A pagan, a person of profound corruption, may do acts externally conforming to the demands of the law. The internal motivation, however, is that of selfish interest or what the theologians call "enlightened self-interest," a motive that is not in harmony with the Great Commandment. Our external deeds may measure up to the external demands of the law, while at the same time our hearts are far removed from God.

Consider the example of a person driving his automobile

within the context of legal speed limits. A person goes on a trip from one city to another, passing through a diversity of zones with differing speed limits. For cruising on the highway, the speed limit is established at 70 miles an hour; for moving through a suburban community's school zone, the speed limit drops to 25 miles an hour. Suppose our driver has a preference for operating his vehicle at a speed of 70 miles an hour. He drives consistently at the speed he prefers. While driving on the highway, his activity is observed by police officers, who note that he is driving in exact conformity to the requirements of the law, giving the appearance of the model safe driver and the upstanding and obedient citizen. He is obeying the law, however, not because he has a concern for the safety and well-being of others or out of a motive to be civilly obedient, but because he simply happens to enjoy driving his car at 70 miles an hour. This preference is noted when his car moves into the school zone and he keeps the accelerator pressed down, maintaining a speed of 70 miles an hour. Now, as he exercises his preference, he becomes a clear and present danger, indeed a menace, to children walking in the school zone. He is driving 45 miles an hour over the speed limit. His external obedience to the law vanishes when the law conflicts with his own desires.

The difference between our perception and God's is that

our ability is limited to the observation of external modes of behavior. God can perceive the heart; God alone knows the deepest motives and intentions that undergird our practice and behavior. Legalism is concerned simply with external conformity and is blind to internal motivation.

Perhaps the most deadly and widespread form of legalism is the type that adds legislation to the law of God and treats the addition as if it were divine law. The Old Testament prophets expressed God's fury at this form of behavior, which they regarded as an improper binding of men's consciences where God had left them free. It is a manifestation of man's fallenness to impose his own sense of propriety on other people, seeking mass conformity to his own preferences and adding insult to it by declaring these prejudices and preferences to be nothing less than the will of God. A frequent point of conflict between Jesus and the Pharisees centered on the Pharisees' traditions, which imposed hardships on the people who were bound by these man-made obligations. Jesus rebuked the Pharisees because they had elevated their traditions to the level of the law of God, seeking not only to usurp God's authority but to oppress mankind.

The elevation of human preference to the level of divine mandate is not limited to an isolated group of moralistic Pharisees in the first century. The problem has beset the church throughout its history. Not only have traditions developed that were added to the law of God, but in many cases they became the supreme tests of faith, the litmus tests by which people were judged to be Christians or non-Christians. It is unthinkable in the New Testament that a person's Christian commitment would ever be determined by whether or not that person engaged in dancing, wore lipstick, or the like. Unfortunately, when these preferences become tests of faith, they often involve not only the elevation of nonbiblical mandates to the level of the will of God, but they represent the trivialization of righteousness. When these externals are made to be measuring rods of righteousness, they obscure the real tests of righteousness.

Majoring in Minors

Closely related to the elevation of human traditions to the norm of law is the problem of majoring in minors, which again was modeled by the Pharisees. The Pharisees distorted the emphasis of biblical righteousness to suit their own behavioral patterns of self-justification. Jesus frequently confronted the Pharisees on this point. Jesus said to them, "You tithe mint and dill and cumin, and have neglected the weightier matters of the law: justice and mercy and faithfulness" (Matt. 23:23a). On numerous occasions, Jesus acknowledged that the Pharisees scrupulously obeyed some points of the law. They paid their tithes, they read their Scriptures, they did a host of things the law required—and Jesus commended them for their actions, saying, "These you ought to have done" (23:23b). However, it was the emphasis that was out of kilter. They scrupulously tithed, but in doing so they used their obedience to this lesser matter as a cloak to cover up their refusal to obey the weightier matters of justice and mercy. That distortion occurs today.

Why do we have a perpetual tendency to major in minors? As Christians, we want to be recognized for our growth in sanctification and for our righteousness. Which is easier to achieve, maturity in showing mercy or in the paying of tithes? To pay my tithes certainly involves a financial sacrifice of sorts, but there is a real sense in which it is cheaper for me to drop my money into the plate than it is for me to invest my life in the pursuit of justice and mercy. We tend to give God the cheapest gifts. Which is easier, to develop the fruit of the Spirit, conquering pride, covetousness, greed, and impatience, or to avoid going to movie theaters or dancing? We also yearn for clearly observable measuring rods of growth. How do we measure our growth in patience or in compassion? It is much more difficult to measure the disposition of our hearts than it is to measure the number of movies we attend.

It is also our inclination as fallen creatures to rate as most important those virtues in which we have achieved a relative degree of success. Naturally, I would like to think that my moral strong points are the important ones and my moral weaknesses are limited to minor matters. It is a short step from this natural inclination to a widespread distortion of God's emphases.

One final type of legalism might be called "loopholeism." Loopholeism involves getting around the law by legal and moral technicalities. Again we return to the Pharisees for the biblical model of loopholeism. The Pharisees had a clearly defined tradition about restrictions on travel on the Sabbath day. One was not permitted to travel on the Sabbath more than a "Sabbath-day's journey," which was a certain distance from one's home. If a Pharisee wanted to travel a distance exceeding the limit, he would take advantage of a technical provision in the law allowing one to establish separate residences during the week. He would have a traveling merchant take some articles of clothing or personal possessions, such as toothbrushes, and put them at strategic points along the road. Perhaps at the two-mile mark, the Pharisee's toothbrush would be placed under a rock, thereby legally establishing his "residence" at that rock. With his legal residences defined in two-mile increments along the way, the Pharisee was free to travel from rock to rock—from "residence to residence"—and make his full trip without ever covering more than the prescribed distance from his "home." The Sabbath-day's journey principle was violated shamelessly while technically being protected by the loophole.

Some years ago, Gail Green wrote a book describing the sexual behavior patterns of American college woman. Dr. Green maintained that the prevalent ethical principle at that time was the "everything but" philosophy. Many forms of sexual activity were considered legitimate as long as the woman stopped short of actual intercourse. It seems almost naive today to think of a generation of college students who embraced an "everything but" philosophy, as those lines have fallen away since then. The point is that the "everything but" philosophy was an example of technical loopholeism, where a person could be a virgin in the technical sense yet be involved in all sorts of premarital and extramarital sexual acts.

Antinomianism Rejects Law

As legalism distorts the biblical ethic in one direction, so antinomianism distorts it toward the opposite pole.

Antinomianism simply means "antilawism." As legalism comes in many shapes and sizes, numerous subtle forms of antinomianism may be delineated. We are living in a period of Christian history where antinomianism is rampant in the church.

The first type of antinomianism is libertinism, the idea that the Christian is no longer bound to obey the law of God in any way. This view of the law is often linked with the cardinal Protestant doctrine, justification by faith alone. In this view, one understands justification by faith to mean that after a Christian is converted, he is no longer liable in any sense to fulfill the commandments of the law. He sees his justification as a license to sin, excusing himself by arguing that he lives by grace and not by law and is under no obligation to follow the commandments of God.

Roman Catholic theologians in the sixteenth century expressed a fear of just such a distortion of the biblical concept of justification. They feared that Martin Luther's insistence on justification by faith alone would open a floodgate of iniquity by those who would understand the doctrine in precisely these terms. The Lutheran movement was quick to point out that though justification is by faith alone, it is by a kind of faith that is not alone. Unless the believer's sanctification is evidenced by true conformity to the commandments of Christ, it is certain that no authentic justification ever really took place in him. Jesus stated it this way: "If you love me, you will keep my commandments" (John 14:15). Christ is a commandment-giving Lord. If one has true justifying faith, he moves diligently to pursue the obedience that Christ demands.

A second type of antinomianism may be called "Gnostic spiritualism." The early Gnostics, believing they had a monopoly on spiritual knowledge, plagued the Christian community. Taking their name from the Greek word *gnosis*, which means "knowledge," they claimed a superior sort of mystical knowledge that gave them the right to sidestep or supplant the mandates given to the Christian community by the apostolic Word. Though Gnosticism as a formal doctrine has passed from the scene, many subtle varieties of this ancient heresy persist to this day. Evangelical Christians frequently fall into the trap of claiming that the Spirit of God leads them to do things that are clearly contrary to the written Word of God. I have had Christians come to me and report behavioral patterns that violated the commandments of Christ, but then say, "I prayed about this and feel at peace in the matter." Some have committed outrages against the Spirit of truth and holiness by not only seeking to excuse their transgressions by appealing to some mystical sense of peace supposedly delivered by the Holy Spirit, but by actually laying the blame for the impulse of their sin at the feet of the Spirit. This comes perilously close to blasphemy against the Spirit and certainly lies within the boundaries of grieving the Spirit. The Spirit of God agrees with the Word of God. The Spirit of God is not an antinomian.

A third example of antinomianism that made a profound impact on the Christian community in the twentieth century was the rise of situation ethics. Situation ethics is frequently known by another label, the "new morality." To identify this theory with one individual would be a distortion. Dietrich Bonhoeffer's work *Ethics*, Emil Brunner's *The Divine Imperative*, and Paul Lehmann's *Ethics in a Christian Context* all have contributed to situation ethics. Bishop John A. T. Robinson of *Honest to God* fame and Bishop James Pike have also entered this discussion. However, Joseph Fletcher, in *Situation Ethics*, has done more to popularize this theory than anyone else.

"There are times when a man has to push his principles aside and do the right thing." This St. Louis cabbie's remark is indicative of the style and mood of Fletcher's book. Likewise, Fletcher quotes a Texas rancher whose story is told in *The Rainmaker* by M. Richard Nash: "You're so full of what's right, you can't see what's good." This rancher is one of the heroes of Fletcher's book.

The general basis for situation ethics is that there is one and only one absolute, normative ethical principle to which every human being is bound—the law of love, a law that is not always easy to discern. Fletcher realized that the word *love* is "a swampy one."

Fletcher argues that there are three basic approaches to ethical decision making: legalism, antinomianism, and situationism. He defines legalism as a preoccupation with the letter of the law. The principles of law are not merely guidelines to illuminate a given situation; they are directives to be followed absolutely, preset solutions, and you can "look them up in a book." He charges that Judaism, Roman Catholicism, and classical Protestantism have been legalistic in this sense. He points to such episodes of crass legalism in church history as the burning of homosexuals at the stake during the Middle Ages.

Antinomianism has no regard for law. Every decision is purely existential. Moral decisions are made in a random and spontaneous fashion. Fletcher sees that the legalist has too many maxims and the antinomian has none. Thus, he maintains that situationism is a middle ground for a more workable ethic. The situationist treats with respect the traditional principles of his heritage, but he is always prepared to set them aside if, in a given situation, love seems better served by doing so.

Fletcher distinguishes between principles and rules: principles *guide* while rules *direct*. In working out applications of the law of love, he sets up the following working principles to serve as guidelines:

1. *Pragmatism*—the good and the true are determined by that which works.
2. *Relativism*—the situationist avoids words such as *never*, *always*, *perfect*, and *absolutely*. (The basic drift of secular man is to deny the existence of any absolutes. Fletcher asserts that there is one absolute as a reference point for a "normative relativism.")
3. *Positivism*—particularized, ad hoc, to-the-point principles. The situationist is not looking for universals; his affirmations are posited, not deduced. Faith propositions are affirmed voluntarily rather than rationally, being more acts of the will than of the mind. We cannot prove our concept of love. The end product of our ethic is a decision, not a conclusion.
4. *Personalism*—ethics deals with human relationships. The legalist is a "what-asker": what does the law say? The situationist is a "who-asker": who is to be helped? The emphasis is on people rather than on ideas or principles in the abstract.

We still have the question, "What do we ask ourselves in order to discover what love demands in a given situation?" How do we protect ourselves from a distorted view of love? Fletcher offers four questions to consider:

1. *The end*: For what result are we aiming?
2. *The means*: How may we secure this end?
3. *The motive*: Why is that our aim?
4. *The consequences*: What forseeably might happen?

All of these need to be considered before an ethical decision can be made.

Positives and Negatives of Situation Ethics

There are some positive aspects of this system of situation ethics; some of the principles involved are commendable. First, situation ethics is not absolute relativism. It is a normative ethic, a kind of absolutism. The limitation to one absolute facilitates decision making and eliminates a certain paralysis of the person who is considering many absolutes.

One of the most important insights that situation ethics offers us is that ethical decisions do not take place in a vacuum. They are made in very real and often painful contexts.

Those contexts must be considered. The high value placed on love and on the worth of persons is also a commendable trait of this position.

However, there are some serious inadequacies in this approach. Underlying the debate between orthodox Christianity and the situation ethicist is the question of the normativity of God's revelation in Scripture.

Fletcher oversimplifies the distinctions between and the definitions of legalism, antinomianism, and situationism. Legalism is a distortion of absolutism. Even Fletcher is an absolutist, though with just one absolute, and all of the legalistic dangers of absolutism are present in his system. One could easily obey the law of love legalistically. If this law is divorced from his context, legalism could easily emerge.

Why, when one holds more than one absolute, is the charge of legalism leveled? Haven't the situationists been simplistic and reductionistic in arbitrarily choosing love as the only absolute? God has laid more than one absolute requirement on man. There is nothing in reason or revelation that should cause one to isolate love as the only absolute. When questioned, these men appeal to Scripture and the teachings of Jesus and Paul. However, they are quite selective about their appeal to Scripture, falling into the quandary of the ethically arbitrary.

The most serious deficiency of Fletcher's system is the problem of how we determine what love demands. We agree with the principle that one should do what love demands. However, Fletcher has problems in determining these demands. Certainly the Bible teaches us to do what love commands, and the content of love is defined by God's revelation. Doing what love demands is the same as saying, "Do what God commands." If we obeyed the Scriptures like a sterile book of rules, we would be legalists. However, if we see the Bible as being the revelation of the One who is love, then we must take seriously what love has commanded.

We know that we are fallen, that we are given over to vices, that we can never perfectly read our own motives, that we are limited to foreseeable consequences, and that we can never comprehensively analyze the ends and the means. Thus, when we face an ethical decision, we find ourselves in a very precarious situation *if* we have rejected the Bible as normative revelation. God has not left us to make these decisions with unaided reason.

In Ephesians 5:1–3, we are given an imperative as followers of God:

Therefore be imitators of God, as beloved children. And walk in love, as Christ loved us and gave himself up for us, a fragrant offering and sacrifice to God. But sexual immorality and all impurity or covetousness must not even be named among you, as is proper among saints.

Here the biblical ethic is on a collision course with situationism. To be a follower of God is an absolute. At no point, in no situation, are we permitted to leave off the following of God. We are to walk in love, the kind of love embodied in the sacrificial ministry of Christ. Love stands here as an absolute—a norm. Its absolute call on us, however, is not left entirely to the situation. The apostle immediately adds an absolute application to it involving sexual immorality, uncleanness, and covetousness. He says, "Let it *not once* be named among you" (KJV). Paul falls into Fletcher's definition of legalism by making a universal prohibition. The apostle falls into the absolute realm of the "never."

Situationism stops with the injunction to walk in love. It must then allow for certain situations where sexual immorality is not only permitted but preferred. If love "demands it" in a given situation, then sexual immorality must be practiced. How perilous is this "guideline," particularly in light of man's most ancient ploy of seduction, "If you love me, you will. . . ."

It is difficult to conceive of concrete situations in which idolatry would be virtuous or coveting would be an expression of love. For this reason, we need to hear Paul's concluding admonition: "Let no one deceive you with empty words, for because of these things the wrath of God comes upon the sons of disobedience" (Eph. 5:6).

Antinomianism by Another Name

Situationism makes the precepts of God relative, leaving us with the mandate to walk in love but to figure it out for ourselves by means of the guidelines of pragmatism, relativism, positivism, and personalism. At this point, situationism is exposed as a virulent form of antinomianism masquerading as a legitimate option between legalism and antinomianism. We cannot realistically expect legalists to call themselves legalists or antinomians to plead their guilt before the world. Though Fletcher protests to the contrary, the substantive elements of antinomianism are rife in his thought.

The Christian ethicist asserts that not only does the Bible require us to do what love demands, but it reveals quite precisely at times what love demands. We have direct instruction in the Scriptures. We are not left with illuminators, but with divine commands.

Consider certain of the Ten Commandments from the standpoint of situationism:

"You shall have no other gods before me," unless it would be the loving thing to do.

"You shall not make for yourself a carved image," unless, on the basis of foreseeable ends, means, motives, and consequences, love would be best served by making a carved image.

Consider Daniel's dilemma (Dan. 6). He could have refrained from praying to God. Certainly the people needed his leadership. What good could he do God's people in the lions' den? Should he have sold out the people and left them without God's agent of revelation for a simple principle of prayer? The end that he wanted was survival. His means were to obey the king. His motive was to serve the people of God. The foreseeable consequences were that some people might be disappointed, but he would be able to make up for that by being a leader and guide to them. So Daniel should have received the blessing of God for doing the loving thing and abstained from prayer to his God.

One of the distinguishing features of the true people

of God is not legalism but fidelity, trust, and obedience to God. Obeying the law to love God is not legalism. When we consider Christ's obedience to God and to the law, it seems impossible not to regard situationism as a serious heretical distortion of the biblical ethic.

There is a principle in the biblical ethic that is rarely seen in the writings of the situationists. They fail to emphasize, as does the Bible, that doing what love demands, what Christ commands, often brings unspeakable suffering. It means enduring radical humiliation and counting one's life as nothing for the exaltation of Christ. It may mean spending a life rotting in a cell in a concentration camp rather than violating the commandment of Christ.

Christ's statement about love is our norm: "If you love me, you will keep my commandments." The proof of our love is obedience to Christ's commandments. Situation ethics establishes a false dichotomy between love and obedience. Situation ethics fails because it does not take love seriously enough.

We turn our attention now to specific questions of ethics that have become particularly controversial in our times—questions of materialism, capital punishment, war, and abortion.

Chapter Four

THE ETHICS OF
MATERIALISM

Materialism is a controversial issue in the church today. Several groups have made this a central issue of debate, speaking of materialism not in a metaphysical sense but in an economic sense: the worldview that places the accumulation of material things at the zenith of private and corporate concern. The pursuit of wealth is seen as the highest good in materialism.

At the other end of the spectrum is a view called

spiritualism, or better, idealism, which sees that only spiritual values are worthy of human pursuit.

The Scriptures repudiate both of these positions. Though material things are not the highest good, neither are they intrinsically evil. There is no room for radical asceticism or monasticism in the church, as these positions deny the world and creation. It is important to recognize that in the old covenant and in the new, many of God's redemptive promises relate to creation; they are promises of the redemption of the physical world. The promise to Abraham and to his seed includes at its heart the promise of land and the promise of prosperity.

The principle of private property is pivotal to discussions of materialism. Many have argued that some kind of communal living or equal distribution of wealth is the only acceptable Christian norm, based on the presupposition that the concept of private property is illegitimate for the Christian. However, the concept of private property is inseparably related to the creation ordinance that sanctifies labor. Karl Marx did something of inestimable value by making it impossible to conceive of the history of man without considering the immense influence of man's labor and the fruit of his labor on his development. This is not to endorse Marxism but to recognize the crucial relationship between man and his labor. When man involves himself in labor, he is behaving as one made in the image of God.

The sanctity of labor is established first by the labor of God Himself in creation, which shows that labor is a duty and a blessing, not a curse. The curse that has been attached to labor since the fall has to do with the quality of the work and the difficulty of the labor by which we bring forth fruit. The thorns and the sweat, not the work itself, are the curse. Pre-fall man labored as much as post-fall man, and that labor produced fruit, which he had the right to enjoy.

Even since the fall, we have no indication that private property (the fruit of one's labor) is condemned or prohibited by God. The first liturgical acts observed in the Old Testament are Cain and Abel's offerings (Gen. 4:1–5). The offerings were legitimate because each man gave from what actually belonged to him. The offertory system of the Old Testament makes no sense when divorced from the system of private property. The right of human ownership is something God has assigned as part of our covenant partnership with Him in creation. Though all human ownership is answerable to divine ownership in the long run, this does not invalidate the concept of private property.

Examining the Decalogue (Ex. 20:1–17), we see that private property is assumed in several situations. The prohibition against stealing presupposes private property, as does the prohibition against covetousness.

We can get a better understanding of the relationship between labor and property by examining the Sabbath commandment. One of the things that is often overlooked is that the commandment not only concerns itself with the seventh day but with the first six: "Six days you shall labor" (Ex. 20:9). The day of rest makes no sense apart from the six days of labor preceding it.

The sanctity of labor is the basis for private property. In both the old and new covenants, the call to labor is an emphatic one, bringing forth fruit as its just reward. The avoidance of labor is regarded as sin. Paul commands labor as an ethical norm. Idleness has no place in the New Testament ethic. In 2 Thessalonians 3:12, Paul says that all people should "earn their own living." In 1 Timothy 5:8, Paul adds that lack of provision for one's household makes one worse than an unbeliever.

Two important conclusions may be drawn from these statements. First, there is the right of private property as the fruit of one's labor. Second, there is the responsibility of honest and diligent labor. Because we live to the glory of God, we have the responsibility to render an honest day's labor. Our labor must not be simply for the acquisition of wealth, but for the glory of God.

Does Scripture Permit Wealth?

This raises the problem of wealth, that is, the accumulation of material goods beyond the level of necessity. Are we permitted to earn and keep more than we need? We are indeed. The possession of wealth is nowhere condemned in either the Old Testament or the New Testament. The means of acquiring wealth are clearly regulated: exploitation, fraud, dishonesty, oppression, and power politics are all condemned. Prosperity and wealth are seen as an aspect of God's providence. This is one of the reasons why covetousness is such a weighty matter. When I covet, I am protesting against God's distribution of wealth. Abraham was perhaps one of the richest men in antiquity. Noah and Job were both wealthy men. God never condemns this wealth, but legitimizes the passing of the wealth from generation to generation by means of inheritance. The patriarchal blessings, which pass on the material blessings, are part of the messianic redemptive promise, including the promise of land.

In the New Testament, we encounter wealthy men who

are praiseworthy. Note the care of the body of Christ after the crucifixion by Joseph of Arimathea, obviously a man of means.

The New Testament does say that wealth imposes severe temptations. Jesus' statement about the camel going through the eye of a needle indicates that a rich man who would enter heaven faces a huge task (Luke 18:25). Practically speaking, the maintenance and protection of wealth takes time and concentrated energy. The parable of the rich fool (Luke 12:13–21) illustrates the perils of preoccupation with riches. It is easy for the rich man to confuse his priorities. But it is also easy for the poor man. It is not merely the rich who are susceptible to the siren song of materialism; its seductive power crosses all socioeconomic borders.

What about the Christian's responsibility to the poor? This, of course, touches the heart of the matter of materialism. Obviously, the provision for some of the needs of the poor is a Christian responsibility. In the Old Testament, some of the needs of the poor were met by laws that included provisions for gleaners (e.g. Lev. 19:9–10). The New Testament also addresses this matter. The collection of provisions by the Gentile Christians for famine-struck Jerusalem was one of the most notable and dramatic episodes in the first century (Rom. 15:25–27). Paul praised both the Corinthian and the

Philippian churches for their generosity. When my brother is in need, I must attempt to meet that need.

Who Are the Poor?

"The poor you always have with you" (John 12:8). This statement by Jesus has been taken by some as license to neglect the poor, as if Jesus were saying, "Oh, well, we always have poverty in our midst, so don't worry about it." Jesus recognized the perpetual plight of the poor, not to ignore it, but to call the Christian community to constant diligence in dealing with the problem.

In identifying the poor described in the Bible, we can distinguish at least four major categories of poor people. What follows is a brief description of each group.

1. *The Poor as a Result of Slothfulness.* The Bible speaks of those who are poor because they are lazy, refusing to work. This indolent group receives sharp criticism from God and comes under His holy judgment. Karl Barth listed sloth as one of the primary and foundational sins of man, along with pride and dishonesty. It is to the slothful that God says, "Go to the ant, O sluggard; consider her ways" (Prov. 6:6), shaming the lazy by telling them to look to insects for instruction. It is this group Paul undoubtedly has in mind

when he says, "If anyone is not willing to work, let him not eat" (2 Thess. 3:10).

Since the Bible criticizes the lazy poor, some have jumped to the conclusion that indolence and poverty are synonymous. Some assume that poverty is always and everywhere a sign of sloth. Thus, the poor can be righteously shunned as they are left to suffer their "just penalty for sloth." Such an attitude reflects a woeful ignorance of or callous disregard for distinctions the Bible forces us to make. There are other reasons for poverty.

2. *The Poor as a Result of Calamity.* The Scriptures recognize that many are left in poverty because of the ravages of disease or disasters. The man born blind, the person left crippled by an accident, the farmer whose crops have been destroyed by flood or drought—all of these have just cause for their impoverished estate. These people are victims of circumstances not of their own making. For these poor, the Bible adopts an attitude of compassion and genuine charity. It is the responsibility of the people of God to see to it that the suffering of these people is ameliorated. They are to be a priority concern of the church. These are the hungry who are to be fed, the naked who are to be clothed.

3. *The Poor as a Result of Exploitation.* These poor are

oppressed. These are the masses who are frustrated daily by their inability to "fight city hall," the ones who live out the mournful slogan, "The rich get richer and the poor get poorer." This group suffers indignities when they live in societies where the social and political institutions, and especially the judicial systems, favor the rich and the powerful and leave the poor without advocacy. Such was the condition of Israel in the eighth century BC, when God thundered against His people. The Word of God came via prophetic criticism that demanded justice and righteousness in a time when the poor were being sold "for a pair of shoes." This was Israel's status when in bondage to Egypt. This kind of poverty moves God Himself as He hears the cries and groans of His oppressed people and says, "Let my people go!" Such injustice and inequity should always move God's church. This is the church's basis for necessary and legitimate social action.

4. *The Poor as a Result of Personal Sacrifice.* These poor people are designated by the New Testament as being poor "for righteousness' sake." This group, whose chief representative is Jesus Himself, is made up of people who are voluntarily poor. Their poverty is a result of a conscious decision to choose lifestyles or vocations with little or no financial remuneration. This class of poor is promised

special blessings from God. They are poor because the priorities of their lives may not mesh with the value standards of the culture in which they live. Those in this class have included Jonathan Edwards, writing in almost microscopic print in order to conserve paper because of his meager stipend (ultimately costing the church and universities hundreds of thousands of dollars to retrieve and reconstruct the priceless treasures of his words); Martin Luther, forgoing a lucrative career to wear the habit of the monk; or the modern businessman who passes up the windfall deal because he has scruples about hidden unethical elements.

What can we learn from these four designations? In the first instance, we should be warned not to lump all the poor together in one package. We must resist the tendency to generalize about poverty. An equally insistent warning must be voiced about the same kind of unjust grouping of the rich. It would be slanderous to maintain that all rich people are corrupt, as if all riches were achieved through evil means or through exploiting the poor. Not all rich people are avaricious or ruthless. To indict the rich indiscriminately would be to condemn the likes of Abraham, Job, David, and Joseph of Arimathea.

Second, we must avoid a theological glamorizing of poverty. Throughout church history, there have been repeated efforts to make poverty the precondition for entrance to the kingdom. It has been seen as a form of works righteousness whereby the poor have an automatic ticket into heaven. This substitutes justification by poverty for justification by faith.

Third, we must recognize that God cares deeply about human poverty and the consequent suffering. Our duty is to be no less concerned than God Himself. As long as the poor are with us, we are called to minister to them, not only via charity, but by seeking and working for the reformation of social and political structures that enslave, oppress, and exploit.

The Responsibility of Stewardship

The basic principle regarding wealth is the principle of stewardship, the truth that a man is responsible for what he does with what he receives. He is not called to liquidate his assets; he is called to give as the Lord prospers him. The characteristic of Christian living is not communism but charity.

The New Testament word for stewardship is the Greek *oikonomia*, from which we derive the English term *economy*. It comes from a combination of two Greek roots, *oikos*, which means "house," and *nomos*, which means "law." Literally, *economy* means "house rule." In antiquity, the steward was not the owner of the house but its manager. He was responsible for the care and oversight of the house. Biblical economics recognizes God's ultimate ownership of the earth and man's duty to manage the earth responsibly.

Economics is not a neutral science divorced from ethical considerations. Economics involves questions of stewardship, the use of wealth, and private and public decisions of value, all of which impinge on ethics. Each time we make a value judgment or render a decision to make use of material goods, we have made an ethical decision. That God is concerned with the material well-being of the world is axiomatic. Man has been called to be a steward of the earth.

The science of economics has become so complex in our day that it has obscured some of the primary principles found in the Scriptures. Though the Bible is not a textbook on economics, it does set forth basic principles that touch upon economic endeavor. As already mentioned, the Bible clearly sets forth the right of private property. However, in addition to this right we also see a concern for equity, for industry, and for compassion. It is not by accident that virtually every major economic system in Western culture has appealed at one point or another to the Bible for its sanctions. Historical capitalism tends to emphasize the principles of private property, equity, and industry, while sometimes neglecting the responsibility for compassion. On the other hand, socialistic forms of economics have emphasized compassion, at times obscuring the rights of private property and undermining the importance of industry and equity. The socialist's ultimate goal is not equity but equality. That is, the socialist seeks a transfer society with the ideal of an egalitarian or equalized distribution of wealth. The goal is noble and virtuous; we would expect that in an idealized society, every member would have equal participation in the wealth of the society. However, we live in a fallen world, where the only way we can have equality of economic welfare is to shut our eyes to the biblical principle of equity. To achieve equality, we would have to penalize the higher wage earners by taking their goods and distributing them to those who have been less-than-responsible stewards or whose skills and services are less valued, financially, by others. Such a principle does violence to the biblical notion of justice.

If we look at the most elementary principles of economics, we see a causal nexus, a formula that must not be violated if we are to grapple with the economic issues of our day. The formula may be seen in the following diagram:

MAN'S MATERIAL WELL-BEING

↓

PRODUCTION

↓

TOOLS

↓

INVESTMENT CAPITAL

↓

PROFITS

We see that there is a causal relationship among these factors. The single most important ingredient for man's material well-being is production. If we are going to feed the hungry, clothe the naked, and give shelter to the homeless, we must be able to produce the goods necessary to meet these needs. Man's physical life is dependent on production. Unless we produce food, we will starve. Unless we manufacture clothes, we will be naked. Unless we build homes, we will be shelterless. God cares about the human body as well as the human soul, and so production becomes a vital ethical concern for Christians.

If we follow our causal reasoning and ask what is the single most important ingredient for production, we would answer "tools." Marx was astute in his understanding of the central significance of tools to man's capacity for production. The reason a peasant in an underdeveloped country cannot produce as much food as a farmer in the industrialized West is not that the body of the Western farmer is stronger, but that the Western farmer has at his disposal labor-saving devices that increase production. More than any other single factor, the machine has been responsible for the explosion of man's ability to produce.

The next question we raise is, "What is the most important single ingredient for the acquisition of tools?" It is not that tools are not available in the world to be used by underprivileged persons, but rather that those without money cannot purchase the tools they need for increased production. Tools cost money to build, to buy, and to maintain.

Where does one get the money to purchase tools? The needed capital is what we would call surplus capital. Surplus capital is a result of profits. Thus, profit is the single most important ingredient necessary for capital to be available to buy tools, to increase production, and to increase the material welfare of a nation.

However, the term *profit* has become virtually an obscenity in the vocabulary of modern man, particularly among Christians. What we often fail to take into account is that the profit motive is not restricted to large industrial corporations or the rich tycoons of industry. The profit motive is at the heart of all economic exchange. The goal or purpose of economic exchange is always and everywhere profit. This statement may appear outrageous on the surface, but let us take a moment to examine its implications.

When a business transaction takes place—when a customer buys a pair of shoes, for example—who realizes a profit? Often the answer is that the shoe salesman or the owner of the shoe store makes the profit. However, the shoemaker cannot make a profit unless first the customer considers it profitable to buy the shoes. The business transaction takes place when the customer values the shoes more than he values the money he must pay for them. Then trade takes place. The customer trades his money for the shoemaker's shoes. The shoemaker, in turn, can exchange that money for other goods that he values more than the money. Thus, in any business transaction, the goal is mutual profit. Both sides must profit or the exchange will not take place, unless the exchange is made necessary by some form of external coercion. This principle is based on the fact that material values are subjective to the extent that not every person values everything to the same degree.

The man who has a surplus of shoes but a lack of food will be eager to make a trade with the man who has a surplus of food but needs shoes. In the transaction, one man values shoes more than meat, while the other values meat more than shoes. A trade opportunity exists because both people stand to "profit" from the exchange.

Profit is good in the sense that it is necessary for the whole community of mankind to survive in a relationship of mutual interdependence. No man is altogether self-sufficient. Each person is dependent to some degree on the gifts and talents of production of other people. The marketplace is where these gifts and talents are exchanged—a place of mutual profit, if the coercive dimension is absent. It is from the surplus of profit that tools can be purchased, production increased, and the general wealth of a nation strengthened. Christians must remember this lest they become participants in schemes by which surplus capital is siphoned off and redistributed in a way that quenches the ability of a nation or a community to be productive.

The protection of private property is so vital to the biblical ethic that we have repeated prohibitions and sanctions against stealing. However, stealing can happen in a multitude of ways, some of which are very subtle. The outright grabbing and carrying off of another person's property is an obvious form of stealing, but stealing can also be accomplished through fraud, by failing to live up to contracts, by using false weights and measures, or even by intentional debasing of currency within a society. All of these means receive the severe indictment of God. One of the most subtle forms of theft is one that is perpetrated through the political system. When people use the power of the ballot box to vote for themselves subsidies from the general coffers, it is a sophisticated form of stealing. For example, if three people live together in a town and one is more wealthy than the other two, the two persons of lesser wealth can conspire to pass a law forcing the wealthier person to distribute his goods to them. Here the power of political force is used to strip the wealthy man of his wealth and distribute it to the other two, who have voted for themselves this particular distribution of wealth. Christians need to be sensitive about how they use the power of the ballot.

Chapter Five

THE ETHICS OF CAPITAL PUNISHMENT AND WAR

The issue of capital punishment has been so volatile that it has set Christian against Christian, church against church, conservative against conservative, and liberal against liberal. The problem is complex, touching the deeper question of the value, dignity, and sanctity of human life.

Any study of capital punishment must begin with an understanding of the primary function of government as ordained by God. Romans 13:1–7 is the classic text concerning God's ordination of government. This text is the most comprehensive and emphatic statement that the Scriptures give us regarding the notion that the power of government is rooted in the ordination of God. It is important to note that the apostle is not speaking here of a theocratic state but of secular government. The text reads as follows:

Let every person be subject to the governing authorities. For there is no authority except from God, and those that exist have been instituted by God. Therefore whoever resists the authorities resists what God has appointed, and those who resist will incur judgment. For rulers are not a terror to good conduct, but to bad. Would you have no fear of the one who is in authority? Then do what is good, and you will receive his approval, for he is God's servant for your good. But if you do wrong, be afraid, for he does not bear the sword in vain. For he is the servant of God, an avenger who carries out God's wrath on the wrongdoer. Therefore one must be in subjection, not only to avoid God's wrath but also for the sake of conscience. For because of this you also pay taxes, for the authorities are ministers of God, attending to this very thing. Pay to all what is owed to them: taxes to whom taxes are owed, revenue to whom revenue is owed, respect to whom respect is owed, honor to whom honor is owed.

The governing authorities are understood to be ordained by God. We are not permitted to obey only those authorities that we consider to be legitimate. It is a *de facto* matter, not a *de juro* matter. God certainly does not endorse everything civil magistrates do, but He does give them certain rights and requires our obedience to them. No government rules autonomously. All civil authorities must, and ultimately will, answer to God. We have the responsibility of obeying even corrupt governments except under certain conditions. Civil obedience is required repeatedly by the Word of God. The principle that governs our right and responsibility to disobey civil authority is this: we must obey those in authority over us unless they command us to do what God forbids or forbid us to do what God commands.

Biblically, God has given two basic rights to governments: the right to levy taxes and the right of coercion so as to maintain order and justice (the power of the sword).

Government was made necessary and legitimate because of the fall of man. The state was ordained to be God's deputy minister for the primary purpose of the restraint of evil. The first appearance of government in the Bible is found in the opening chapters of Genesis, when Adam and Eve were expelled from the garden and consigned to live east of Eden. The entrance to the garden was barred by the presence of an angel with a flaming sword. Here we see the appointment of a ministering agent, namely, the angel who was equipped by God with an instrument of restraint and was granted the power of coercion, symbolized by the flaming sword.

The central duty of government is to enforce the laws that are designed to restrain evil. Augustine said, "Sin is the mother of servitude and is the first cause of man's subjection to man." Augustine argued that government is a necessary evil, in fact, an evil made necessary by the presence of evil in the human heart. It is because men are prone to violating each other that government is established to check the strong and ruthless who exploit and oppress the weak and the innocent. Government is necessary because men do not live to the glory of God, loving Him with all their hearts and their neighbors as themselves. The only ultimate alternative to government is anarchy, in which each man lives for himself. Thus, God instituted government as an act of His grace to protect the weak and the righteous from the wicked. The authority of the state is not an intrinsic authority but one that is derived from the authority of God.

The Power of the Sword

The issue of capital punishment emerges when we examine the right of the state to bear the sword. In the first instance, the sword is seen as an instrument of coercion. I once had a conversation with a United States senator who said to me, "No government ever has the right to coerce its subjects to do anything." I was shocked by the senator's statement and replied, "Senator, you have just stated that no government has the right to govern." The power of coercion is the essence of government. Perhaps the simplest definition we can find for government is the word *force*. In a very real sense, government is force. If you take away the government's right to coerce, you take away the government's right to govern, leaving the government with the impotent authority of rule by suggestion. The power of the sword is the arm of the government we call law enforcement, without which the law represents merely a list of suggestions. God did not give the sword to the civil magistrate as a means of intimidation only by rattling. In biblical categories, "the power of the sword" is an idiomatic expression to indicate the power to kill.

At this point, the issue of capital punishment comes to the fore. In the Bible, we first read of the institution of capital punishment in the narrative of creation. In the garden, there was one restraint, one prohibition given to man. The clear-cut punishment for disobedience of this command was instant death. "In the day that you eat of [the tree] you shall surely die" (Gen. 2:17b). It is important to note that when man sinned, God did not invoke the full measure of the punishment for disobedience. Indeed, capital punishment came upon the race, but it was postponed in terms of its implementation. Originally all sin was regarded as a capital offense. Capital punishment was the divine judgment for any and all sin. However, God reserved the right to replace justice with mercy according to His own prerogatives. Because God has not executed that punishment consistently and immediately—except on rare occasions, such as the cases of Nadab and Abihu (Lev. 10:1–3), Uzzah (2 Sam. 6:1–8), and Ananias and Sapphira (Acts 5:1–11)— the world tends to take God's mercy for granted. In some circles, capital punishment is considered to be cruel and unusual punishment for any crime.

In the old covenant, God reduced the number of capital offenses and limited the penalty to approximately thirty-five specific crimes. The New Testament exhibits an even more gracious dispensation, with a further reduction of capital offenses.

Before the institution of the law at Sinai, we have an

even more important statement, found in the covenant God made with Noah. Here we see a covenant that renews the ordinances of creation, a renewal of God's rule for man as man. There is a certain sense in which the laws of this creation covenant are of far broader import than even that legislation found in Israel or in the New Testament. Here God proposes legislation for man as man, not for man as Jew or man as Christian. Man *qua* man is the one who receives the stipulations of the covenant of creation. It is therefore significant that capital punishment for murder is built into creation and presumably is binding as long as creation is intact. The renewal legislation is found in Genesis 9:6: "Whoever sheds the blood of man, by man shall his blood be shed; for God made man in his own image." This text is a command, not a prediction. The sanction is clear. If a person murders another person, God requires that the murderer be put to death by human hands.

It is ironic that both sides of the dispute on capital punishment tend to base their arguments on the principle of the sanctity of life. The humanist argues that human life is so valuable that we are never justified in taking another person's life. From a biblical perspective, the humanist view actually reflects a lower view of the sanctity of life than that found in Genesis 9:6. From the vantage point of the twenty-first century, we tend to view the Old Testament society as severe and savage, forgetting that it already manifested an enormous reduction in capital offenses. As noted above, the New Testament brought an even more gracious policy, not because God changed His mind and saw that His former policies were too cruel and severe, but partly because the responsibility for the execution of justice in the New Testament moved out of the hands of the theocratic state and into the hands of the secular state.

The question of how many crimes are considered "capital" in the New Testament is open to lengthy debate. The only crime that we can be certain is a capital offense is first-degree murder. In the Decalogue of the Old Testament, there is a clear prohibition against murder. The penalty for transgressing the prohibition in the Ten Commandments, "You shall not murder," was capital punishment. However, the broader legislation of Mount Sinai included several distinctions with respect to degrees of murder. The establishment of the cities of refuge, for example, dealt with the problem of involuntary manslaughter.

It is ironic that many have appealed to the Ten Commandments as a basis for repudiating capital punishment, taking the prohibition "You shall not murder" as a universal mandate. This comes from a superficial reading of the Sinaitic legislation and a failure to observe that within the context of the Sinai covenant the penalty for violating that commandment was death. The holiness code of Israel clearly called for the death penalty in the case of the murder of another human being. The murderer must forfeit his own life. The reason given for the special sanctity of human life was that man is created in the image of God. God is concerned with preserving the work of His creation, and at the top of His priorities is the preservation of the life of man. There is a sense in which the commission of murder is regarded by God as an indirect assault on Him. Just as an attack on an ambassador of a king is seen as an affront to the king, so the act of murder is an assault against the very life of God, inasmuch as it desecrates one made in God's image. It is important to understand that power over life is not rescinded in the new covenant but is mentioned again in Romans as a prerogative of the state. Thus, the Scriptures uniformly assert the propriety of capital punishment in the case of murder.

When we apply the principle of capital punishment to a given society or to a given culture, we must be careful lest we plunge into the matter without considering other ramifications of the biblical sanctions. Though capital punishment was imposed in the Old Testament, it was circumscribed by other principles that were very important to the justice process. In the Old Testament, justice was truly blind under the law. The rich were to be given no special privileges before the bar of justice. That ideal exists in our own society, but at a practical level there are too many circumstances in which Lady Justice peeks or removes her blindfold altogether to take note of the rich and the powerful who are her suitors. Under the old covenant, no one could be convicted of a capital offense on the basis of circumstantial evidence. Two or three eyewitnesses were required, and their testimony had to agree. If the witnesses who testified in a capital trial were found guilty of perjury, the penalty for bearing such false witness was itself death. There is no question that we need reforms to protect against inequities of the application of capital punishment in our modern culture, but when we object to capital punishment in principle, we are objecting to a sanction God Himself ordained.

The Ethics of War

The issue of a Christian's involvement in war is an extension of the more primary question of capital punishment. In a certain sense, war is capital punishment on a grand scale. It involves the civil magistrate's widespread use of the power of the sword. Basically, there have been three foundational positions taken regarding war in Christian history:

1. Activism
2. Pacifism
3. Selectivism

Activism is a simplistic approach that views all wars as permissible. It reflects the position that the subjects of the state are to give absolute obedience to the civil magistrate regardless of the situation. It reflects the cliché, "My country, right or wrong." This is an uncritical approach that has little to do with the biblical ethic.

Pacifism, on the other hand, says that all wars are wrong and all people's involvement in war is wrong. The pacifist view would restrict Christians from participating in any kind of war.

The third position, selectivism, maintains that involvement in some wars may be justifiable. It is within the context of selectivism that the just-war theory has emerged in Christian history.

A sophisticated argument by pacifists who are Christians is based on the ethical mandates Christ gave His people, whereby He prohibited the Christian from the use of retaliatory violence and uttered a clear prohibition against building His kingdom with the sword. The pacifist transfers these prohibitions from the sphere of the church to the sphere of government. Not only is the private citizen or the ecclesiastical authority forbidden the use of the sword, but the state as well. Some divide the question by admitting that the state has the power of the sword, but Christians are not to participate in the state's function. The question that is raised immediately is, "On what grounds would a Christian refuse to obey a civil magistrate who calls him to do something for which there is no biblical prohibition?" If God commands the state to bear the sword and the state conscripts the Christian to help with that task, on what moral grounds could the Christian refuse to comply?

The Swiss theologian Emil Brunner has remarked: "To deny on ethical grounds the elementary right of the state to defend itself by war simply means to deny the existence of the state itself. Pacifism of the absolutist variety is practical anarchy." Helmut Thielicke has added his judgment that pacifism is a moral cop-out. He draws a parallel between pacifism and a situation where the Christian witnesses a murder and allows it to happen without interference. Thielicke argues that it is our responsibility not only to minister to a man who has been mutilated by robbers, such as the man going down to Jericho, but to love our neighbor by preventing the crime as well.

Selectivism holds that involvement in a war may or may not be wrong. The particular circumstances and situations must be evaluated on each occasion to discern which side, if either, has a righteous cause to defend. The victim of a clear-cut act of aggression would have the right of self-defense, according to the selective view.

Chapter Six

THE ETHICS OF ABORTION

Abortion is a monumental issue that ignites heated debates. Divisions in the state and in the church are many, with major denominational church bodies coming down on both sides of the issue. The fires of controversy show no signs of abating.

In dealing with this issue, three major questions must be answered:

1. What is abortion?

2. Is abortion right or is it wrong? Or is it possibly without moral bearing?
3. Does the church have the right to advocate civil legislation on this question? Some church bodies have advocated a "middle way" under the rubric of "pro-choice," arguing that this should be a matter of conscience, not of civil legislation, and that it is wrong for the state to prohibit abortion.

The Biblical Basis for Discussion

No teaching in the Old Testament or New Testament explicitly condemns or condones abortion. Exegetically, the debate has been waged on implicit grounds. The Old Testament passage that has received the greatest attention concerning this matter is Exodus 21:22–24:

> When men strive together and hit a pregnant woman, so that her children come out, but there is no harm, the one who hit her shall surely be fined, as the woman's husband shall impose on him, and he shall pay as the judges determine. But if there is harm, then you shall pay life for life, eye for eye, tooth for tooth, hand for hand, foot for foot.

There is a built-in ambiguity with this text, giving rise to differing interpretations of its precise meaning and application. The theological house is divided between "maximum" and "minimum" positions. The problem centers on the words "there is no harm." To what "harm" does the verse refer? This problem is linked to another, namely the question of what is meant by "her children come out"? Is the text referring to an incident in which the woman, being jostled by fighting men, is induced to a premature childbirth that produces anguish and inconvenience that the law seeks to recompense even though the premature child lives and thrives? Or is the text speaking of a case in which the induced premature birth yields a stillborn fetus, and further considerations come into play only if the mother suffers additional complications, even death?

The Old Testament scholar C. F. Keil adopts the maximum view, arguing that the "there is no harm" clause refers to both mother and child. The idea is that if the premature baby survives, recompense is limited to damages paid for the inconvenience and mental anguish suffered by the mother, as claimed by the husband and awarded by the judge. But if the child is harmed or dies, the full measure of the *lex talonis* (eye for eye) is to apply. In this reading, the unborn fetus is so highly valued by Scripture that the life-for-life principle is applied, and the unintentional causing of abortion in the midst of an unrelated violent act warrants the death penalty. If this interpretation is correct, we would have decisive evidence that Scripture considers the unborn fetus as "life" in the fullest legal sense.

The minimal view of the text argues that the "there is no harm" clause refers exclusively to the mother. Under this schema, the abortion of the fetus would not invoke the *lex talonis* or legally be considered murder or loss of life. Only if further complications affect the mother does the "eye for eye, life for life" equation apply. The inference then would be that Scripture does not regard the fetus as "life." The fetus would be protected by the law, however, and its *value* could be established via a lawsuit. Some push this position further by arguing that though legal indemnities *may* be imposed, they are initiated by the claims of the husband. The unspoken presumption is that the "value" of the fetus is determined to some degree by the subjective values attached by the parents. In this "case," the Scriptures deal with an abortion or miscarriage imposed from without, apart from the design of the parents, who presumably desire the pregnancy to reach its full term. The passage is then made of no consequence to the question of an intentional abortion performed according to the will and design of the parents. The minimal view thus protects the parents and not the fetus.

The differences between these interpretations cover the gamut of the contemporary debate. Though I am convinced of the maximal interpretation, I must admit the problematic and ambiguous character of the text.

In the New Testament, the word *abortion* is used only in a figurative sense. One passage often cited to support an antiabortion stance is Luke 1:39–42, when Mary visited Elizabeth and the unborn John the Baptist "leaped in her womb." Other biblical passages speak of people being conceived in sin and known by God in the womb. The question is whether these allusions are to be taken as religious hyperbole or poetry. However, these passages clearly indicate that God is involved with man's history prior to his birth.

When Does Life Begin?

The question of when life begins has been pivotal to the discussion. Different points on the conception-birth continuum have been proffered, with the added problem of variant medical definitions of "life" itself.

Some maintain that the fetus becomes a person at the moment of birth. There are good reasons for this argument.

This is a rather clear line of demarcation, indicating a new status, a new moment of independent existence with individuation beginning with the snipping of the umbilical cord.

Another view points to the moment of "quickening"; another to the time when the circulatory system is fully developed. Others say that the principle of life in the Old Testament is the "breath" of life in man. Therefore, life is present when the lungs develop and the fetus can breathe on its own.

The moment of conception has been seen by many groups to be the beginning of life, since all the potentiality of personhood is then present. David and others speak of their conceptions as part of their personal history.

What we conceive the fetus to be determines the value we assign to it. There are those who say that the embryo (the term usually used to refer to the product of conception during its first twelve weeks) is nothing more than a blob of protoplasm. Others argue that it is merely a highly specialized form of parasite. It has been compared to a cancer, a tissue growth foreign to the mother, which the body seeks to reject. If the mother fails to reject it, it will be fatal to her.

These are emotive terms that greatly cloud the issue and

represent an irresponsible approach to the question. To refer to an embryo as a "blob of protoplasm" is to be guilty of a severe form of reductionism. The *parasite* term is equally inaccurate, as parasites have an independent life cycle that includes reproduction. As for the analogy to cancer, a cancer left to natural development destroys life. An embryo left to natural development produces life—a difference that cannot be ignored.

The crucial concern here is that we can say with certainty that at any stage of development the fetus is a potential life, a potential human being, with a high level of probability of becoming a human being if left to the normal course of its development. With this in mind, let us look at the essence of the debate: What is the relationship of abortion to the biblical prohibition against murder? Does the Bible have anything to say about the destruction of a *potential* life?

In the Old Testament, there are five distinctions in the broader application of the Decalogue's prohibition of killing, including distinctions for manslaughter and involuntary murder. In the New Testament, however, we have an authoritative application and interpretation of this prohibition.

"You shall not murder" is not a universal prohibition against taking human life in any context, but it is wider in its scope than simple first-degree murder. Jesus' understanding of this mandate included a prohibition against hatred. Hatred is understood as murder of the heart. In effect, Jesus said that the law implicitly prohibits *potential murder*. Left unchecked, hatred results in murder. He said that the law prohibits the *potential destruction of life*. This is not the same as prohibiting the *actual destruction of potential life*. However, these two are very close to being the same, similar enough to raise serious questions about abortion. In terms of the sanctity of life, potentiality was clearly an issue with Jesus.

If we are seriously considering the spirit of the law, we must pay attention to the implications (implicit understanding) of a particular commandment. This means that the converse of a prohibition must be affirmed. The prohibition against wanton destruction of life is an implicit command to promote the sanctity and safeguarding of life. The sanctity of life is the supreme basis for the prohibition of murder. The question is, "Does the sanctity of life include concern for potential life?" There is no way we can prove decisively that it does. However, in light of the overwhelming concern in the Scriptures for the safeguarding and preservation of life, the burden of proof must be on those who wish to destroy potential life.

Arguments in Support of Abortion

Perhaps the strongest case for the support of liberal abortion laws is the right of the mother. Some groups have countered this with the issue of the right of the unborn. But the root of the matter goes deeper. The issue biblically is between the concept of the woman's right and the woman's responsibility. Does the woman have the right to disrupt natural law? Is she responsible for the natural consequences of her voluntary acts? Relative to this debate is the fact that we do not have absolute rights over our own bodies within the sphere of creation. Self-mutilation is forbidden within the Old Testament. If mutilation before conception is wrong, what about mutilation after conception?

Another argument used to support legalized abortion is the utilitarian argument, which opts for the lesser of two evils. The argument is that under the present restrictions, the only abortions that are available (apart from therapeutic abortions) are those obtained illegally, which are often hazardous. To protect people from their own foolish acts, wisdom would dictate legalizing abortion. This argument is irrelevant to the question of whether or not abortion is right. Committing a felony is also a dangerous business, but the danger is no justification for the legalization of bank robbery.

The issue of therapeutic abortions must be dealt with separately. Generally they are used in two situations: where there is clear and present danger to the life and physical health of the mother, and where there is concern for the psychological well-being of the mother, especially in the case where the woman has been victimized by a rapist. In the first instance, there are two basic points. Some argue that in the case of danger to the life of the mother, it is better to destroy the fetus to save the mother. The actual life is more valuable than the potential life. Others say the fetus should be saved, basing this on the matter of certainty versus probability. Suppose that the death of the mother is 99 percent probable if the child is left to be born. If there is an abortion, that means 100 percent certainty of death for the fetus. If there is one chance in 100 for both to survive, this group holds that the chance should be taken.

The final question is that of church and state. Many Christians have taken the position that it is not the church's business what the state legislates, since the church is not to legislate morality. However, the state *does* have the responsibility of legislating morality. Traffic laws deal with the moral issue of how one drives one's car. Justice is a moral issue; laws are an attempt to promote justice. The essence of legislation is morality. The church has the responsibility to speak to the legislature. The state's primary function is the preservation of society and the preservation of life. When the state is involved in legislation that does not respect and promote the sanctity of life, the church must speak out. While we recognize the separation of power between church and state, we cannot recognize the autonomy of the state before God. The state is also a servant of God. If there is any legislation on which the church has the responsibility to speak, it is on this one, since the heart of the issue is the sanctity of life.

Evaluating the Third Option

The debate within the church tends to focus on the *tertium quid*, the third option, known as the "pro-choice" position, one that has steadily grown in popularity.

Evidence is emerging that the strategy of pro-abortionists, led by Planned Parenthood, is the oldest strategy of all: "divide and conquer." Mainline Protestant bodies have been solicited to aid the cause of abortion on the grounds that human rights are being violated by the oppressive tyranny of the monolithic Roman Catholic Church. Eager to stand against tyranny and for human rights, countless Protestant clergy and denominations have endorsed the middle ground between the pro-life and pro-abortion poles. The *via media*, or moderate middle, has been defined as the pro-choice position.

Two vital questions must be faced by those wrestling with the premier moral issue of our day. The first question is, "What is the practical difference between the pro-abortion and pro-choice positions?" In terms of legislation, a vote for the pro-choice stance is a vote in favor of abortion, which the pro-abortionists understand clearly. No one knows the exact figures, but it is obvious from polls that a large group of voters, if not a plurality of them, favor the middle ground. Certainly it is this middle position that has swung the balance of legislative power and the weight of public opinion to the side of the pro-abortionists. We hear it said repeatedly, "I would not choose to have an abortion, but I think every woman has a right to make that choice for herself."

In this statement the focus is on the concept of a human "right." The mother is said to have the right over her own body to bear a child or to dispose of the fetus. (The central issue is not about victims of rape or mothers endangered by childbirth; the issue before us is abortion on demand for convenience.) This presses the second question: "What constitutes a moral right and from whence come moral rights?"

As Christians, we recognize, I hope, that there is a profound difference between a moral right and a legal right. Ideally, legal rights reflect moral rights, but such is not always the case. How does one establish the moral right to choose abortion? From the law of nature? From the law of God? Hardly. Natural law abhors abortion and divine law implicitly condemns it.

The real basis of the right to choose abortion is want. The unspoken assumption of the pro-choice position is that I am free to choose whatever I want—an assumption repugnant to both God and nature. I never have the moral right to do evil. I may have the civil and legal right to sin but never the moral right. The only moral rights I have are to righteousness.

Is not the issue more complex? Does it not hang together with the broader issue of the extent of government intrusion in our private lives? Surely it does. I know few stronger advocates of limited government than myself. I abhor the proliferating tendrils of government pressing into our lives. However, the primary purpose of government, biblically, is to exercise restraint on mankind in order to promote, preserve, and protect the sanctity of life. This is the very *raison d'être* of human government.

If abortion on demand is evil, no one has the moral right

to choose it. If it is an offense against life, the government must not permit it. The day is being captured by those in the moderate middle who have not faced the ethical implications of this position. This is the moral cop-out of our day—the shame of our churches and her leaders. It is time to get off the fence. To be pro-choice is to be pro-abortion. Be clear about that and abandon the muddled middle.

Chapter Seven

ETHICS AND THE
CONSCIENCE

The function of the conscience in ethical decision making tends to complicate matters for us. The commandments of God are eternal, but in order to obey them we must first appropriate them internally. The "organ" of such internalization has been classically called the conscience. Some describe this nebulous inner voice as the voice of God within. The conscience is a mysterious part of man's inner being. Within the conscience, in a secret hidden recess, lies the personality, so hidden that at times it functions without our being immediately aware of it. When Sigmund Freud brought hypnosis into the place of respectable scientific inquiry, men began to explore the subconscious and examine those intimate caverns of the personality. Encountering the conscience can be an awesome experience. The uncovering of the inner voice can be, as one psychiatrist notes, like "looking into hell itself."

Yet we tend to think of the conscience as a heavenly thing, a point of contact with God, rather than a hellish organ. We think of the cartoon character faced with an ethical decision while an angel is perched on one shoulder and a devil on the other, playing tug-of-war with the poor man's head. The conscience can be a voice from heaven or hell; it can lie as well as press us to truth. It can speak out of both sides of its mouth, having the capacity either to *accuse* or to *excuse*.

In the movie *Pinocchio*, Walt Disney gave us the song "Give a Little Whistle," which urged us to "Always let your conscience be your guide." This is, at best, "Jiminy Cricket theology." For the Christian, the conscience is not the highest court of appeals for right conduct. The conscience is important, but not normative. It is capable of distortion and misguidance. It is mentioned some thirty-one times in the New Testament with abundant indication of its capacity for change. The conscience can be seared and eroded, being desensitized by repeated sin. Jeremiah described Israel as having the "brazen look of a prostitute" (Jer. 3:3, NIV). From repeated transgressions, Israel had, like the prostitute, lost her capacity to blush. With the stiffened neck and the hardened heart came the calloused conscience. The sociopath can murder without remorse, being immune to the normal pangs of conscience.

Though the conscience is not the highest tribunal of ethics, it is perilous to act against it. Martin Luther trembled in agony at the Diet of Worms because of the enormous moral pressure he was facing. When asked to recant from his writings, he included these words in his reply: "My conscience is held captive by the Word of God. To act against conscience is neither right nor safe."

Luther's graphic use of the word *captive* illustrates the visceral power the compulsion of conscience can exercise on a person. Once a person is gripped by the voice of conscience, a power is harnessed by which acts of heroic courage may issue forth. A conscience captured by the Word of God is both noble and powerful.

Was Luther correct in saying, "To act against conscience is neither right nor safe"? Here we must tread carefully lest we slice our toes on the ethical razor's edge. If the conscience can be misinformed or distorted, why should we *not* act against it? Should we follow our consciences into sin? Here we have a dilemma of the double-jeopardy sort. If we follow our consciences into sin, we are guilty of sin inasmuch as we are required to have our consciences rightly informed by the Word of God. However, if we act against our consciences, we are also guilty of sin. The sin may not be located in what we do but rather in the fact that we commit an act we believe to be evil. Here the biblical principle of Romans 14:23 comes into play: "Whatever does not proceed from faith is sin." For example, if a person is taught and comes to believe that wearing lipstick is a sin and then wears lipstick, that person is sinning. The sin resides not in the lipstick but in the *intent* to act against what one believes to be the command of God.

The dilemma of double jeopardy demands that we diligently strive to bring our consciences into harmony with the mind of Christ lest a carnal conscience lead us into disobedience. We require a redeemed conscience, a conscience of the spirit rather than the flesh.

The manipulation of conscience can be a destructive force within the Christian community. Legalists are often masters of guilt manipulation, while antinomians master the art of quiet denial. The conscience is a delicate instrument that must be respected. One who seeks to influence the consciences of others carries a heavy responsibility to maintain the integrity of the other person's own personality as crafted by God. When we impose false guilt on others, we paralyze our neighbors, binding them in chains where God has left them free. When we urge false innocence, we contribute to their delinquency, exposing them to the judgment of God.

Further your Bible study with *Tabletalk* magazine, another learning tool from R.C. Sproul.

....

Sign up for a free 3-month trial of *Tabletalk* magazine and we will send you R.C. Sproul's *The Holiness of God*

TryTabletalk.com/CQ

About the Author

Dr. R.C. Sproul is the founder and chairman of Ligonier Ministries, an international Christian discipleship organization located near Orlando, Fla. He also serves as copastor at Saint Andrew's Chapel in Sanford, Fla., as chancellor of Reformation Bible College, and as executive editor of *Tabletalk* magazine. His teaching can be heard around the world on the daily radio program *Renewing Your Mind*.

During his distinguished academic career, Dr. Sproul helped train men for the ministry as a professor at several theological seminaries.

He is author of more than ninety books, including *The Holiness of God, Chosen by God, The Invisible Hand, Faith Alone, Everyone's a Theologian, Truths We Confess, The Truth of the Cross,* and *The Prayer of the Lord*. He also served as general editor of the *Reformation Study Bible* and has written several children's books, including *The Donkey Who Carried a King*. Dr. Sproul and his wife, Vesta, make their home in Sanford, Fla.